Homage

By Kathleen Spivack

Copyright © 2024 Kathleen Spivack

Book Design by Steve Glines
Text ITC Garamond
Titles University Roman
Cover Photo: Maria Lane

ISBN 978-1-7331185-3-8

Wilderness House Press
145 Foster St.
Littleton Massachusetts 01460

To Maria Lane: Steadfast; Courageous;
At Home In The World.

Contents

Ping Pong Sestina: For Elizabeth Bishop
    Ping Pong Sestina. For Elizabeth Bishop   3
    poets great and small   5
    For Anne   6
    Body my engine   7
    The Frost Farm in Derry, New Hampshire   9
    Peace Pilgrim   12
    Madame Joelle Blot, my French Teacher   14
    Tivoli. The Curator Goes Home.   15
    The Great Railroad Train of Art   17

Their Tranquil Lives
    Their Tranquil Lives   23
    Seeming to Happen   25
    Button   26
    The Painter Tries to Explain   27
    Straining   29
    The Lighthouse Keeper   31
    To have and to hold   33
    For George Whitman, Shakespeare & Co. *Paris*   *35*
    There Is a Word or Several, Must Be   40
    Kathleen Spivack   43

Publications – Acknowledgements

Ping Pong Sestina with Elizabeth Bishop –
Written for the Memorial, Poetry Society of America, New York.
With Robert Lowell and His Circle Sylvia Plath, Anne Sexton,
Elizabeth Bishop, Stanley Kunitz & Others,
University Press of New England.
poets great and small – *Kalliope*
The Frost Farm in Derry, New Hampshire – The Real Paper;
Swimmer in the Spreading Dawn, Apple-Wood Books
Peace Pilgrim – *Oberon*
Madame Joelle Blot – *The Southern Review*
Tivoli – New England Poetry Club, first prize
The Great Railroad Train of Art, -*New Guard,*
The Knightville Poetry Contest, judged by C Simic.
Their Tranquil Lives – *First Prize, Allen Ginsberg Poetry Award,*
Patterson Review; A History of Yearning,
The Sow's Ear Chapbook Competition Winner
Seeming to Happen – *Tampa Review*
Straining – *Atlantic Monthly.* Flying Inland
Button – *A History of Yearning,* The Sow's Ear Chapbook winner
George Whitman Shakespeare and Company – *Tumbleweed Hotel*
There is a Word or Several, Must Be - *The Paris Review*

Homage

Ping Pong Sestina: For Elizabeth Bishop.

Ping Pong Sestina. For Elizabeth Bishop

On Monday mornings in your apartment we faced
each other across the net, two poets
having a go at ping pong. Your arthritic hands
gripped the paddle. Determined, you played
against my energy and youth, a tricky game
in which I held myself back, wanting you to win,

not to succumb to your age, or defeat: always to win.
You grinned with delight at the speed of the game,
pressing in for the slow shots, gingerly played
as the ball dripped casually over the edge of the net,
handling your aching body and keeping the poetic
plonk of the white ball going. Wheezing, your face

was childlike. "Please call me Elizabeth." But I couldn't face
that. You were "Miss Bishop." Elizabeth Bishop, Poet,
as in "Miss Bishop's too noble-O." Even with one hand behind
your back, whatever smallest edge you had you played
to advantage as if seeing angles were a game and as if
there were only one way of recording, one way to win

that cancelled all other alternatives. You so easily won
friends, admirers, yet always at play
was your encircled suffering, lack of love hinted, gamely
ignored; the poems and stories in which pain was handled
so far back behind the eyes that the poetry
stood for itself, was really poetry, not pain. You faced

it only obliquely. Once, showing me a photo, the face
of yourself as a baby, small, stubborn, not at all "poetic,"
protesting abandonment in crumpled white lace, hands
tightly folded as if your dear life, even then, was not
a game, as if you sensed you had something dark to play
out, a despairing intelligence behind that winning

little person. But it was late now. You were winded,
fighting arthritis, the ball. I found myself mentally playing
both sides of the table, cheering your game
so much more than my own. Did I hold back? Did I hand
you the final point? The match? No, you won on
your poems alone. Your austere inward face

was wickedly triumphant, handing me the paddle. "Shall we play again?" Lunch was waiting, talk of books and poetry. But facing winter noon in Cambridge, we started another game.

poets great and small

great henry left a hole in the hedge;
so few stalwart trees remain.
sylvia perversely choking herself on bittersweet—
(too much room for the young sprouts.)

falling upon the "thorns of life"
they drove them murderously inward.
and randall sleepwalking, who will be great for us now?
friends, persist, persist in the clearing,
blazing like sumac in the burnt-over meadow.

For Anne

Who can bear the passion in your voice
now that death has stopped the record?
And still you issue from the same worn grooves:
such longing. Such longing!

Friend, from the phonograph you are still wise and true:
you go on talking, wry, amused.
No one could keep you from writing the poem-of-your-death
so I write a poem to your death, as you wanted me to.

Body my engine

1. Body my engine
my joyous tickler.

2. Body:
hugged knees and
the Pony, the do-it, the knobby
desire to please.

3. Body my Knight with that
"K" still in front of that word.
Weight. Wait at the window, stop-start.
White Nights.

4. Body my castle.
The frothy wild steed,
the wind and the ride
of it. Body my pride

5. In its deeds. Your dark hair,
the Yes of the side-saddle ride
past the trees at full gallop:
Hooray for the Here

6. And the forbidden ride
with its blaze-leap inside.
The secretive brushing
of branches: moon tide.

7. I am made Whole.
I am all Hole,

8. With the hips and the tits
of it, yapping of mutts
and their pups
at the wound of it. Trapped.

9. Now relinquish what was.
I enter a tree, trying to hide.
from my own-some,
The pastness. The lonesome

10. disguises. Tamed
body, steadfastness, its costume:
the apron like bandages. Wait

11. Was this what I planned? That
do-it? That dare?
The suppose?
The repair?

12. A bobbin unspooling;
my plodding old
Dobbin, sway backed
knock-kneed, bowed as

13. a rocker: tick-tock.
Salt lick.
The Body muzzled--

One touch,
one final cuddle.

14. This spiraling
Body, a birds-wing. Adrift
on the downdraft.

15. A Feather.

The Frost Farm in Derry, New Hampshire

Robert Frost, your homestead in Derry, New
Hampshire is a mess:
the orchard out back has been cut down;
the ground has been stripped of its topsoil

and is an auto wrecking yard.
In the moonlight the subsoil glitters like Christmas
with cracked windshields; discarded tires
wreathe the mounds where apple trees once stood.

Route 28 passes right out front.
I lay awake, acquainted all one night
with the upstairs front bedroom
where you listened to the breathing of your children

in nineteen oh seven.
Now diesel trucks and souped-up cars shift gears
by the front door. They are more deafening than rain.
There is a trailer camp across the way

where you used to do all that meeting and passing.
The brook's a brown polluted stink.
It's impossible to get hired help;
and they've torn out your kitchen to make it

workable. They have moved in a fellow
who says he is a poet.
But who knows? This poet has a wife
who isn't in the least a silken tent

nor he. Living on food stamps, they are
substantial human beings
who don't know a damn thing
about farming.

A tramp came to the door today,
some bearded hippie from out west named Patrick,
who thinks you're the greatest.
This fellow hitchhiked all the way from Montana

to see this place where you lived and worked.
Now Patrick, the poet and the wife
are sitting in the green remodeled kitchen
in what used to be your farmhouse

and rapping (that's the word
they use these days) about you,
Robert Frost, you lousy farmer,
who sold this farm and got out of New Hampshire

the minute your grandfather's will said you could.
The farm's so mean and poor no one could make it pay
so you did what you could do best which was to write,
(and some of the walls you mended are still standing.)

When you finally sold the Derry farm you wrote:
"It shall be no trespassing/ If I come again some spring
In the gray disguise of years/ Seeking ache of memory here."
The new owner auctioned the topsoil to make the down payment;

later he sold to the auto wrecking yard. That's progress,
I guess. But you were so paradoxical
you were to look back on that hen scratching
in Derry as in an idyll

in a long line of insanities and death.
("What but design of darkness to appall?")
The first child died and was buried in the snow
but four slept still in a safe white whisper.

I should be telling you this in perfect metrics:
an approximation of the heart will have to do.
To suffer so much and still to go on writing
was either famous Frost perversity or courage.

Years later, after your wife had died,
she sent you back with her ashes to scatter them.
You drove up to the door on the highway home
and found the farm scarred by strangers, irretrievably.

And you turned away with the ashes past the house,
past the broken glass, the wreckage, the ruined fields,
and walked out on New Hampshire for the second time,
to sleep in America forever.

Peace Pilgrim

She was eighty some years old
when she finished walking across America:
a little white haired old lady
in pants and a navy blue sweatshirt;
her name written across the back: "Peace Pilgrim."
Her past: she had renounced it,
and all attachments too, focusing
only on her naïve message "peace."
That simple word walked with her:
peace: inner, individual,
in families, community and world—
a childlike faith.
Were things as complicated then?
Or was she crazed? An inspired bag lady
with a cockeyed glint in her bright blue eyes?
A glowing lunatic hobo for which America is famous?
She walked away the latter half of her life,
crossing and re-crossing the country
in a constant state of prayer.
Her real name was unknown:
she had changed it so long ago anyway.
The details of her life, her family,
she said, were unimportant—only what she was doing,
right now, in this glistening moment:
the scent of pine breathing up from the roadside,
rain or scarves of wind against her face,
the clouds that changed about her
yet cradled her heart, a glowing ember
around which the night sky swirled.
She carried a blanket, water, answered her mail,
and slept, saying "Body, lie down,"
by the side of the road, in culverts,
meadows, and on the floors of local jails.
She ate only when offered food, which was
surprisingly often, she said,
spent time with folks along the way,
believed in something she called
"god" and didn't expect anything else.

Surprised, life was the perpetual gift.
Singular in happiness,
she spent her life walking around
peacefully, looking out at the world
in delight, writing about it sometimes,
a harmless little loony old lady
whom one might envy:
Peace Pilgrim.

Madame Joelle Blot, my French Teacher

You gathered lilacs for me, immoral armloads
Of lilacs. Shivering, they groaned as they broke.
They shed some starry petals on wet ground.

We were in Tours, in the Loire Valley, in France, yes
in France, country of excess. You stood on the ladder
hacking away at your voluptuous lilac bush

and hurled the heavy branches down.
You were sixty years old, a delicate curly haired person:
Madame Joelle Blot, my French teacher, determined that

I should not spend another night without lilacs in my room.
Then you mouse-stepped down the ladder, little feet in little
strappy high-heeled shoes, set the lilacs firmly in a crate and

carried them inside, a bushel of lilacs. For me. No one
had ever… Selecting just the exact tool, you laid into the lilacs
with an enormous antique hammer, mashed down the woody

stem-ends splintery and flat. This is how it's done, you showed me.
In France. Where they break eggs to make their omelettes.
In Tours, where they speak the best French, unaccented

and pure, so they say. I wanted to learn that language from you.
I was foreign, foreign even to myself
and so applied myself diligently to your lessons.

Even the lilacs knew you were boss. They glowed in my damp
chamber, lasted for weeks as you said they would,
and flung their weighted perfume recklessly about.

Their daringly giddy fragrance swirled like 'Beginning Again',
like a kiss, like learning the meanings of words one had perhaps
always known: like Possibility. Like Risk.

Tivoli. The Curator Goes Home.

The smoky backdrop
dims to violet and gauze.
This is how death might look
seen from another side,
or perhaps death-in-life.
When they turn off the pretty fountains,
when the painted rooms are closed to you
and the beautiful miniatures
you have collected, cast aside;
when the iron hasps of doors
shut importantly, a heavy final sound,
and the Curator goes home.

And you are left standing as at a dress
rehearsal, backstage, covetous
at the closed gate of your own
life. Perhaps you are old or
handicapped; you are already
becoming invisible behind the curtain,
even to yourself. Absence of water-sound,
unloved, hurts louder than any white-spray
fountain splashing "Look at me!"
What you missed, what you wanted
so much and missed anyhow:
it was all here in this poised expectant

day you tried to enter closed villas
and gardens and couldn't
and found yourselves straining
to hear what was no longer here:
staring outward in a strange manner,
with eyes that were not really
eyes any longer, but carved
parabolas of stone,
marble-lidded, secretive,
constrained by old habits
into assuming life like positions,
tree-like, calcifying,
still harboring longings.
The word "Transfixed" comes to mind.

The Great Railroad Train of Art

"Farewell, little Katya," my Russian Lit. Professor at Oberlin College
called. He was running alongside the train in Cleveland, Ohio.
His little legs churned, his belly pumped in and out.
"Farewell, my little Katya, on the Railroad Train of Art...."
And the great Lackawanna locomotive pulled out of the station
and I graduated from college and the years started
to pass by the train at first distinctly like trees, then faster,
merged into a green smear; became a whoosh of sound sucking
the silver train forward. Is this what was meant by "Perspective:"
College Art History class, yawning in darkness, slides of "Old
Masters" and occasionally too much light, a shocked glare at the end
of the show? There were other travelers, too, on the train, clutching
chickens and boy friends, sleeping through boring parts of Rome,
Florence, and Renaissance Man. And children in baskets, amazed
young girls, and grandmothers no one could startle,
lit by white streetlights by which the train passed
quickly before entering tunnels where, if one opened an eye
one could still see Leonardo up there on full screen,
straining and clawing, trying something new.

We had taken our notebooks and bundles, smoothing them down,
scribbling in a clandestine way. We were special with secrets
and anesthesia was invented and midwives supplanted
by surgeons taking off legs and Michelangelo hacked at his marble
while the train rushed on through violet evenings.
And in Holland a woman set a table and light shone
on the draperies and fruit.
We looked into that quiet room with longing. "Bourgeois,"
my Prof. scoffed, as we pleaded for make-up exams. I was hopeful,
my college diploma, virginity lost to that Russian professor
and now, perhaps, a job. Yes, a job,
typing to the clack of the wheels as the relentless
locomotive thundered on through the Industrial Revolution,
the horrors of Hogarth, the Song of the Shirt.
I typed faster and faster, teaching American children.
At some point the Greeks invented beauty:
Keats called it something else,
and the train puffed through stations steaming like the filthy

ones of Monet. Had we reached
French Impressionism so fast? Had the Curies
already discovered radium? There was no time for a quiz.
"Truth; 'tis all ye need to know." No time.

We passed villages where the stationmaster ran out of his cuckoo
clock office and gaped and the comfort of cows, seen from the
train that never stopped. We envied the peaceful shepherds dozing
at crossroads of Flemish art.
But we were moving faster than Turner's clouds. Smallpox
was cured, Fleming found penicillin in a cave and the train
entered a tunnel. A new tray of slides: Gogol, Pasternak, and Marx
were writing madly, all at the same time.

We passed pine forests, snowfields, and on the smooth white sheets
of marriage, somewhere during the Russian revolution, I made love to
a husband whom I promised to cherish all my days, and birthed
children on the train. And did not throw myself under it.
And other passengers also gave birth, as if during emigration,
lying under that great shawl of silence, hardly crying out;
and our children grew while the train sped away
from the Czar, past the Irish Potato Famine,
toward that Vanishing Point on the horizon:
"O My America, my new found land."
We were going to be taught to plant corn.

And there was sadness too, of course, and bitter words,
(we entered the Depression), and a turning away of the husband.
Outside, the air was lacy with new birch leaves,
everything stretching its arms and crying, *"stop here!"*
And a hunger for love after the Great War,
for all the beautiful young men, roared up like the boundless cry
of the locomotive hurtling toward summits and Yalta, the Axis
powers, death of the Archduke, and promises of collaboration.
They were dancing at Maxim's; and somewhere in here Modern Art
seemed to begin as well as Movies. We were passing towns too
quickly with a dark moaning sound. After Pearl Harbor
and Polio, while Picasso and Braque discovered Cubism,

we petitioned the conductor to slow down. Young women
bared their breasts. Attendants came to us and told us to be quiet;
the porters, respectful with luggage, tipped their caps.
We offered to get psychoanalyzed, (not on the syllabus)
for Independent Study, to go to the Far East, or to gaze
impassively over Great Plains

from the back of a horse.
These requests were denied. This was before Vietnam.
This was before napalm and hippies.
This was before Eleanor Roosevelt *"became a lesbian."*
Khrushchev took off a shoe and everyone invented sex.
And the Great Railroad Train of Art rushed on through modern
history and further, full speed now and uncontrollable.
No one could slow it down though many tried,
wild haired and waving helplessly.
But at Yasnaya Polyana when the train does "*kindly*" stop,
I shall find my Russian Lit. Professor waiting;
he will look exactly as he did.
I'll embrace my parents, loves, and children, hand in
my final bluebook on Tolstoi, whisper "The light, the light.
Turn out the light." And get an A plus for the full course.

Their Tranquil Lives

Their Tranquil Lives

Oh lost world of Gustav Klimt,
the jeweled and doe-eyed women
swam the walls and ceilings
of pre-Holocaust Vienna's
ornate opera. Women's compliance
did not need to be stated,
was pink and white
and not hidden by drapes.

World War I had not yet happened.
The city was a beaker spilling over
with bits of gold applied
which one could drink
or pour into, carefully
lavish and lucky.

Outside the window apples
shone in their dappled garden.
The women had proud
names, and pregnancies.
They rose like mermaids through
their tranquil lives,
upward and passionate.
The insides of their wrists
were white and still unmarked,
smoothed with kisses:

Vienna before History—
Each morning was a waking: pond
drenched in light; the path,
perfumed with little flowers, stitched
white butterflies and the painter-god
creating first-words; a mosaic
of forbidden.

As if memory
would tapestry forever
voyeur-painter's studios, light-
drenched: the livid golden hair
and modeled arms and bracelets lifting:
perfect breasts; rounded nutcracker
thighs and, ready for the
taking, the ripe fruit.

As if the comet,
pleasure, would never
burn itself to ash; the dross,
once-glorious color
seeping, leaching, thinly
staining Europe.
Oh much punished and
lost worlds of Gustav
Klimt, while you stroked
undertone rose-ochre tints
to flesh, your century,
demented, waited
for its urgent re-inventions;
voice-over, take-over
newsreel/newsprint narratives:
blunt black- and- white.

Seeming to Happen

Was it something I chose: the door, open,
the backyard singing with flowers, their upturned faces,
the wide sky beyond that, even that,
and the stranger beckoning "Come"?

Was it this I chose, walking out the kitchen,
letting the dish towel fall, untying the apron?
Were these the apple blossoms, white as in a dream?
Were the horses neighing to me?

Were there messages, as I thought there were, in the tall grasses?
Did even the flowering maple tree hang its head in acquiescence?
Was this myself, stepping out of an accustomed life
Moving toward, and then into, the gleaming arms of a stranger?

Even if the words "stranger" and "danger" rhyme;
Even if in that one gesture, an entire choice has been made;
I, who thought myself "indecisive" find indeed I was only waiting:
Waiting for you, for me, for paths to walk into this painting.

Button

The last time we saw her
she was waving from a doorway
of a boxcar gathering speed
and going east. The last time
we saw her she was carrying
a thin suitcase and a button
was missing from the sweater that
her mother knit: *goodbye, take care of
yourself.* When they took her
she was wondering *where why
why me?* and we were also,
helpless, straining to see beyond
a horizon we would only guess at as
we watched her, small & vanishing,
standing and looking out that one last
longing time at breathing blue-green fields
And why didn't she turn
and run right out of the picture frame
back into our waiting arms
before it was too late, my late
great aunt, a last un-
noticed snip of history?

And that lost button, why
wasn't it sewn on tighter?

The Painter Tries to Explain

I am the plainest shell;
nothing particularly to notice.
There are plenty of others where I come from:
an osteoporosis of the mind
in elliptical striations.
Irritated pulsations of color
and the ocean's sudden stomach heave,
once brought me to a Summer Shore
but washed me home again.

Displayed in the glass jar of
an impermeable European
life; fossilized,
like other shells
among my family's collectibles,
I wonder: can a shell
have feelings? Memory?
The rolled canvases that,
water stained, I brought back
with me will not prove anything.
We are whitish- gray and tawdry.
Sunlit and opulent, Tahiti
seemed an answer, streamed down
through the surface of water and the
jagged lightning bolt of God took aim.
The lurid parrot's orange
screech, vermillion
eyes, hooked yellow beak,
shattered my whorled surfaces;
splashing blind brightness onto
bruised blue shadows under which
a few red horses dreamed.

Watery, I long to undulate
back to that glowing
island shore, carried by
the ocean's breath:
to stroke again the inner petals
of my Hibiscus.
How her long brown
feet trod on my rough edges till her fingers
found and clasped me, treasure, while
her dark eyes sparkled, head thrown back,
white starry flowers in her hair. How I
disappeared into my painting:
how her hands made me special.

Straining

Sojourning alone in Paris,
he thought, now finally
he was a poet. All the props
were his: the cloak, the hat
like a cringing accordion,
the mustache, the walking stick
pronouncing ends-of-sentences
on the sidewalk.

Only he had not reckoned
on the loneliness. Isolate,
terrible as a lavatory,
it chilled him, coming in from
the warm purple streets.
His room lay in the darkness
like a terrapin, promising nothing.

Something unseen, a posterity,
crouched in the corners, watching,
ticking off his movements: his forearms
as he washed his shirt
on the basin; the casual
lighting of a match. That eerie tiger
noticed everything. His neck
prickled at his writing stand.

"If you love me, guard
my solitude," he wrote
to endless mistresses, his wife,
his friends. Solitude!
It is the sallow wallpaper
of furnished rooms.
Worried as a snail, he worked,
extruding a thin slimy track.

While to him a young man
earnestly wrote: Dear Mr. Rilke,
how shall I become a poet,
having a most desperate longing
to do so, and in my bosom
some small songs?

And like a garden, the replies
profused, lavishing
in leaking roses, borders
of bachelor's-buttons, blue
at the buttonhole,
and the scent of solitary
sentry lilies: sentences
burgeoning like blood from a slit
artery.

No tourniquet could staunch it.
The heart, spurting, sprinted
onto one page. "Dear Mr. Kappus…"
Loneliness, that leech obscene
on his mouth, was sucking,
glutting out whole sonnets,
clots of sound.

The Lighthouse Keeper

Enthroned in the glowing
dome of the lighthouse,
the lighthouse keeper sang.
"I am in Paradise.
I live among the birds.
Sometimes I see angels:
I think I am becoming
an angel, drawn in a beam of
light, upward, spreading
hands over water, guiding ships.
If you listen, you can hear birds
also encouraging the sailors,
more benevolent than Ulysses'
sirens." He beamed at us.
"My lighthouse, here
on Cap d'Antibes,
is the most powerful on these
shores. The prisms magnify
even the lightest flicker
of feeling. Every quick thought
darting between here and
Nice is noticed. Sailors pray
to me; mothers and sweethearts
pray. Oh, I am a happy man,"
he said to us, expansively
at the top of the tower at the
crest of a hill on the island
where we had climbed to see
his great light. The keeper
polished the glass. "Regard,"
he enjoined, looking down.
And we did. "Do you see that
small path that goes back through
the woods? Upon leaving,
take that exact route

straight to the sea.
My little birds and angels
will safely guide you there."
He spoke in what sounded
like French. We looked back.
Above us, spikes of gold
flashed, a modern halo.

To have and to hold

and he said to me
live and be happy

coming back coming back

and I heard him in the flowers,
the tender new leaves, little hands
unfolding,

and I heard him in the sky;
the rooftops as in
archetypical
photographs of Paris
and he said to me

live.
Be happy.

Listen, said everything, **give this**
attention. Remember.

that whispering, was it the wind;
the ocean telling its consolations?

the upturned flowers
in simplicity?

new life
unfolding wetly at its mother's
side and opening its eyes?

Understand:
the sadness was finished; the failures;

the night sky
didn't trouble as it once had;

and his sweet swollen
broken body
was made whole again,

entering the cosmos
in a great dust / light / energy / particle / swirl:
the glare and white whoosh of that ***Yes***.

Live and be happy, Kathleen,
he said (as he turned).

And I would.

For George Whitman, Shakespeare & Co. Paris

"Write something for me." George, exuberant, said.
She could not think of anything to say.
There was so much, too very much to say.
She thought of soft books waiting to be read:

how sweet to turn those pages; just to be
at one with work. She saw the kids
who flocked to Paris, sought to write—and did!
All this was in George's vision, energy:

Eccentric, generous. How all roads led
to Shakespeare and Company. Always had. She looked
across the Seine. The vista took
one's breath away: the bookshop; Paris spread

before her; conversation, Notre Dame….
To read, to write, this was a writer's dream.
All this, and more: the writer's rooms, the cat,
the company, including lively Sylvia, she praised.

The tea was poured, the cookies passed. Oh happy days
with George Whitman, Shakespeare & Co. teacups raised.

Lessons from Pablo Casals

1.
With the master stroke of his bow on the open C string
he took on the twentieth century. *I have experienced a crisis of
conscience, my beloved Spain,* he said. *I will stop
playing until there is finally no more war.*

2.
What, no music? No sound of the sonorous
Bach? No satisfying dominants and fifths;
no resolutions? What will be left us
when the concert halls fall empty? What of the
performer crucified on stage?

3.
Auburn hips, tipped women: screams,
discordant sobbing: Schoenberg.
And a silence after music stops when
the last overtone has died away. O children,
in your sweet high voices sing: sing on
past Guernica, Theresienstadt. *I will devote myself
to little birds, the purity of God as he/she should
have/might have been; to justice.*

Each morning, playing Bach he returned to the source.
The open **C** rose from the shuttered windows;
flowers, morning glories, opened their blue eyes
like prayers; celebrations spilled over the balconies.

4.
I want to create an ideal world
in which suffering is banished: in which
I make music with friends, and little jokes, gently.
For this I am willing to be silent if necessary.
Encircling the 'cello, spooning my chest
to her backside, our twinned beings resonate with music.
I <u>am</u> music. This is as close to singing
as I can get. *Yes. This is my song to you.*
Listen: this passage falling away into C minor. Listen.

5.
Who are you that you write about me?
I am *Kathleen,* once your student, & the student of
your student who was my 'cello teacher in America.
The girl who wouldn't talk, who let the 'cello,
great blonde imposition, speak for her. Who wanted to be
an expressive instrument, vaguely, for God and peace
and universal love, whose chest resonated to "great
ideals," who wanted music to stand for her own
small suffering, who mingled her sound during
World War Two; who wanted to sing: I am that girl.
The hands must not shake!

6.
Lugging the 'cello, an ant with a bread crust,
up the large hill to my music lesson, my music teacher,
like every other 'cellist, resembled you: short, bear-cub
build, requisite musician-hair plastered over the bald spot
and rounded shoulders in permanent servitude. *Charmed
afternoons slid down delicate eighth notes into darkness.*

7.
After the violet hours, after supper with my teacher
and perhaps more music, afterwards who could not, carrying her
'cello and scrawled school books go home hopeful into the night?
Into dark adolescence, into a cold house where all
was silent, into wordless trepidation, absences
in corners while the fictive "end" of the Second
World War became the "Cold War," inner/
outer. The kitchen clock ticked furiously, the only
sound in the hollow rooms; a metronome, abandonment.
"Mein Gott, no! It must sing. Make it sing! Ta **Taaaah!** *Like this!"*

8.
Preparations for playing the 'cello: squeezing
a tennis ball to strengthen the hand. Memorizing a score.
Hammering the fingers down silently, over and
over onto the throbbing strings. My bow
skittered before the 'cello
section's entrance; fingers anxious in the solo
places, bent and struggling; *"Amateur,"* a word
for a clumsy lover. *Here the tempo changes. "La laaaaaa,"
he swanned, and moved my elbow, showed me.*

9.
A displaced young girl tells her sorrows to her violoncello
in America while in Puerto Rico, *not in Catalan,* Senor
Pablo Casals plays silence to the birds. Palm trees triangulate
the sea, open like fans their frond-like fingers, stretching the span
of an octave, open A to high A sharp to the fretted harmonic. *Eeee*

10.
And from the phonograph your "Unaccompanied Bach,"
unfolds, a Calla lily. *"You must play the first note with authority,"*
you said. *"Daaah. da da da da dah dah*
Duuuuuuh,"* sternly as your forearm drew the bow across the strings:
majestic gleaming demonstration; maple-bellied sound.

11.
Exile in Puerto Rico where the mother was born in the same
house where your wife was later born: coincidence?
The Birds of Paradise opened their wide throats, singing neon
paeans; lizards skittered along the white washed walls:
the fingers thick & stubby, *spatulate.*

12.
Each morning you began the *Anna Magdalena Bach* book,
parting shutters, opening windows, sliding back the curtains,
heavy linen on their wooden rings, music occupying doorways,
balconies and terraces, the magenta garden spilling downward.
Thirsty hills rose to the passages like rain.
Their fragrance, sostenuto, stayed like after-notes:
you at the window, encircling the 'cello, haloed by sun,
by unheard memories: stroked sound.

13.
Those perfect oval notes, smoke rings, as from the Times Square
"Camels" sign, still wreathe my room. Like memories, they make
a space in now- historic air. The record turns. Music has weight,
evanescence; dust motes seek their tonal resolution.
Shall I ever attain such certainty; a life lived for belief?

*The New York Philharmonic string players took their students
to Toms River, New Jersey, where they ran a summer music
camp. Pablo Casals, who was in residence and coached us young
teenagers.*

There Is a Word or Several, Must Be

Breathe these words in all languages before they're lost, thank you
and mean it. The things we take for granted and now have aban-
doned us. Or will. Water, air, rich earth beneath the rubble, thank
you for our daily breath. Give us this day. Exhale the little thank you
words they're quick, slip out our pores, clean hair. A shower. Soap
and aspirin. Thank you. Whoever "you" might be. Appreciation.
A survival skill we never get to hone enough. Thank you. For life.
For health, for the newborn baby slipping out between the hips.
For wondrous eyes and little rosebud fists, thank you, sweet pea.
And jump ropes, patience, teachers of the world, and teach me self-
control. Migration, vanishing, the butterflies the orange peach of
the oriole. Whatever bright eyed bird you once saw flicker past
and wondered what was that? You were lucky to have it show itself.
You are lucky perhaps to be it, plumage, proud breast and wings.
Thank you for shelter, the blanket of morning. Of this morning.
When first frost found naked earth, or when you found that one
shade tree in the desert of last summer. Sun like a knife-blade,
now the reluctant release of pain, those precious moments when
it goes away. Do you still remember having such moments?
There is a word or several, must be, in all the languages for saying,
thank you in a world of swirl. Thank you for not yet abandoning me,
my body. Wait a bit. Yes please.

Kathleen Spivack

KATHLEEN SPIVACK is the author of many books of poetry and prose. Her publishers include Doubleday, Graywolf, A.A. Knopf, The Scarecrow Press (Poets Now) nominated for a Pulitzer Prize, Sow's Ear, Applewood Books, Earthwinds Editions, University of New England Press, and others. Her poems have been published in large and small journals and magazines from The New Yorker, The Atlantic to Happiness Holding Tank. She has won numerous Solas Best Travel Awards for essays. She has received notable prizes: two Fullbright, Discovery, Byrdcliff, National Endowment for the Arts, Two Radcliffe Institute and Bunting Fellowships, several Massachusetts Foundation and Council, The Allen Ginsberg/Patterson, and American Academy in Rome, etc. for her work. She's been at many artist retreats including McDowell, Yaddo, Karolyi, and Ragdale. Like most writers, she has had lots of rejection too.

The newspaper Cleveland Plain Dealer gave her an award in 1957 for the best student editorial writing. This enabled her to come to Boston as an undergraduate to study with Robert Lowell. Lowell forgot that he had agreed to take on this Oberlin student and passed her on to "the women" – Elizabeth Bishop, Sylvia Plath, and Anne Sexton. She became Lowell's student and lifelong friend. She later wrote a book about her experiences with these poets, particularly how they dedicated themselves to their work *With Robert Lowell and His Circle: Sylvia Plath, Anne Sexton, Elizabeth Bishop, Stanley Kunitz, and others,* (University of New England Press).

A novel *Unspeakable Things* (A.A. Knopf) takes place chiefly in the NY Public Library and details the adventures of a Viennese immigrant family during World War II.

Kathleen has taught at Ecole Polytechnique, Boston University, Brandeis, Harvard University, Université de Paris VI and VII, Université de Versailles and many writing workshops: Aspen, D.H. Lawrence Ranch, Ghost Ranch, International Women's Writing Guild, Paris WICE, Radcliffe Alumni Workshops, and others. She performs her work widely.

www.ingramcontent.com/pod-product-compliance
Lightning Source LLC
Chambersburg PA
CBHW071801040426
42446CB00012B/2659